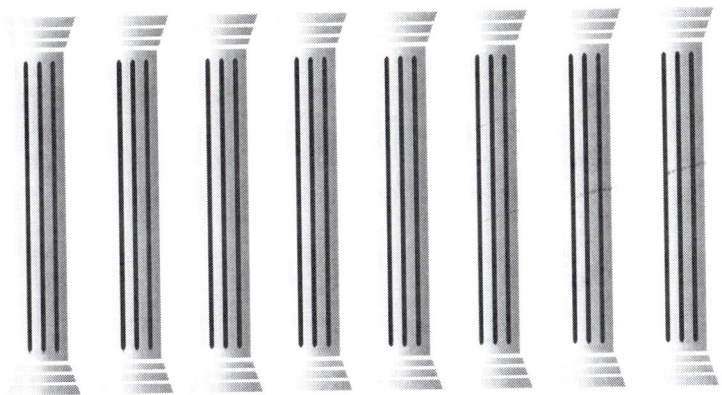

Zen
and the Art of Fundraising

8 Pillars of Success

Alexandra Pia Brovey, JD, LLM

I could hardly put down this book. Through accessible descriptions of Buddhist principles, stories of donor meetings, and even interactions with her dog, Alex takes you, the layperson, planned giving officer, or general fundraiser, on a journey of both professional and personal enlightenment.
Claudine A. Donikian, JD, MBA
President/CEO and Chief Marketing Officer of Pentera, Inc.

Charitable gift planners of all stripes, both newly minted and experienced, should read and take this book to heart. It's written by a gift planning master and is extraordinarily well-written.
Jonathan Tidd, Esq.
Attorney

Alex turns the heart and soul of many donor scenarios into lessons and finds key principles to share. This isn't about money or tax deductions, but rather it's a focus on impact and expressing one's morals, values, and beliefs.
Christopher Kelly
Director of Development, Planned Parenthood, Michigan

Whether you are a beginner fundraiser or a seasoned practitioner, you're going to love this book. Packed with practical tips along with stories of how NOT to close a gift, it is the source of valuable wisdom from an exceptional gift planning veteran.
Margaret M. Holman
President, Holman Consulting, Inc.

This book will inspire you to kick over a few conventions and achieve real fundraising mastery.
Steven L. Meyers, PhD
Author of *Personalized Philanthropy: Crash the Fundraising Matrix*

In the beginner's mind, there are many possibilities. In the expert's mind, there are few. That insight from Zen practice is a conundrum for gift planners, who are challenged to climb a mountain of technical detail that they can probably never summit. The most effective gift planners are deep experts AND perpetual beginners. They know that every encounter with a new person, or reunion with a familiar one, is full of possibility. Alex reminds us how to keep our beginner's minds open, while our expert minds are doing math and remembering rules and regulations.
Barbara Yeager
Director of Operations, National Association of Charitable Gift Planners

Zen and the Art of Fundraising: 8 Pillars of Success

Alexandra Pia Brovey, JD, LLM

Published by
CharityChannel Press, an imprint of CharityChannel LLC
424 Church Street, Suite 2000
Nashville, TN 37219 USA

CharityChannel.com

Copyright © 2018 Alexandra Pia Brovey

All rights reserved. No part of this book shall be reproduced, stored in a retrieval system, or transmitted by any means, electronic, mechanical, photocopying, recording, or otherwise, without written permission from the publisher. No patent liability is assumed with respect to the use of the information contained herein. This publication contains the opinions and ideas of its author. It is intended to provide helpful and informative material on the subject matter covered. It is sold with the understanding that the author and publisher are not engaged in rendering professional services in the book. If the reader requires personal assistance or advice, a competent professional should be consulted. The author and publisher specifically disclaim any responsibility for any liability, loss, or risk, personal or otherwise, that is incurred as a consequence, directly or indirectly, of the use and application of any of the contents of this book. Although every precaution has been taken in the preparation of this book, the publisher and author assume no responsibility for errors or omissions. No liability is assumed for damages resulting from the use of information contained herein.

ISBN Print Book: 978-1-938077-99-9

Library of Congress Control Number: 2018936037

13 12 11 10 9 8 7 6 5 4 3 2 1

Printed in the United States of America

This and most CharityChannel Press books are available at special quantity discounts for bulk purchases for sales promotions, premiums, fundraising, or educational use. For information, contact CharityChannel Press, 424 Church Street, Suite 2000, Nashville, TN 37219 USA. +1 949-589-5938.

Publisher's Acknowledgments

This book was produced by a team dedicated to excellence; please send your feedback to Editors@CharityChannel.com.

We first wish to acknowledge the tens of thousands of peers who call CharityChannel.com their online professional home. Your enthusiastic support for CharityChannel Press is the wind in our sails.

Members of the team who produced this book include:

Editors

Acquisitions: Steven Meyers

Comprehensive Editing: Stephen Nill

Copy Editing: Stephen Nill

Production

Layout: Stephen Nill

Design: Stephen Nill

Administrative

CharityChannel LLC: Stephen Nill, CEO

Marketing and Public Relations: John Millen

About the Author

Alexandra Pia Marie Brovey has been a full-time fundraiser and charitable gift planner for almost two decades and an estate planning attorney for twenty-five years. She graduated from The Pennsylvania State University in 1990 with a BA, *summa cum laude,* Phi Beta Kappa; Georgetown University Law Center in 1993 with a JD; and University of Miami School of Law in 1995 with an LLM in Estate Planning.

After practicing law full-time for six years, Alex joined Penn State as a planned giving officer where she worked for five years, visiting with alumni and friends around the country. After relocating to New York, Alex worked as Senior Director, Planned and Major Gifts at Pace University and later as Senior Director, Planned Giving at Stony Brook Foundation, before joining Northwell Health Foundation in 2008 as Senior Director, Gift Planning. She currently leads a team that supports twenty-three hospitals, a world-renown research institute and a medical school in the greater New York City metropolitan area.

Alex is a leader in the gift planning community. She joined the Pittsburgh Planned Giving Council before cofounding the Central Pennsylvania Planned Giving Council and serving as Vice President. Upon relocating to New York, Alex joined the Philanthropic Planning Group of Greater New York, serving in a multitude of leadership roles, culminating in her current roles as President Emeritus and mentor. She is a member of the Charitable Estate Planning Council (Long Island, NY) and a member of the Nassau County (New York) Estate Planning Council.

At the national level, Alex served as a cotrustee of the Legal Advocacy Fund of the American Association of University Women, after serving as Vice President, Membership for the State College, Pennsylvania branch. She served as a board member and treasurer of the National Association of

Charitable Gift Planners and is currently serving a two-year term as chair of the Leadership Institute.

Alex enjoys speaking around the country on a variety of legal and philanthropic topics. She has had articles published in *Trusts and Estates, Planned Giving Today, Charitable Gift Planning News, Fundraising Success Advisor,* and the *Journal of Gift Planning.*

Alex earned a black belt in Shotokan karate in 2015. She is a proud Penn State Lifetime Alumni Association Member and serves as a career coach. Alex has interviewed prospective law students for Georgetown Law for over a decade. She coached junior soccer for five seasons, and enjoys visiting national parks, reading, and solving puzzles.

Dedication

I dedicate this book to my husband, Ed, and my sons, Noah and Gabriel, who I love very much. I also dedicate this book to all the donors whose generosity enabled me to pursue a career in gift planning and who strengthened my pillars.

Author's Acknowledgments

I want to acknowledge my Northwell Health Foundation Gift Planning team, Shawn T. Mroz and Hazel R. Paulino, my colleagues at Northwell Health Foundation, and my former colleagues at The Pennsylvania State University, Pace University, and Stony Brook Foundation. I give special thanks to my publisher, Stephen Nill, JD, for his support and our fun conversations throughout the process. I warmly thank Steven L. Meyers, PhD, whose friendly smile years ago on a shuttle ride sparked a conversation during which we both shared a dream to someday write a book. Steven achieved his dream, and he inspired me to achieve mine.

I thank the following colleagues and friends for reviewing my manuscript: Claudine A. Donikian, JD, MBA; Margaret M. Holman; Christopher Kelly; Steven L. Meyers, PhD; Jonathan G. Tidd, Esq.; and Barbara Yeager.

I thank my parents, Esther and Dan, for sharing the author gene. I also thank my sisters, Jennifer and Allison, for their support, encouragement, and feedback. I look forward to reading *their* books someday.

I lovingly acknowledge my husband, Edward G. Capps, to whom I have been married for over twenty years, for his patience as I worked my way through ten karate belts, three laptops, and numerous meditation sessions (including on a few vacations). I thank my precious sons, Noah and Gabriel, for sharing their cool gaming headphones, as well as for their pride and love.

Although they cannot read this book, I am grateful to my three Bernese Mountain Dogs—Ferguson, Leopold, and Napoleon—who would alternate between nudging me and sitting patiently on or near my feet for hours, from when I first dreamed about writing a book through having my first one published.

Contents

Foreword xxi

Introduction 1

Chapter One 3
Introduction to Zen

Chapter Two 9
The First Pillar: Being in the Moment

Chapter Three 15
The Second Pillar: Listening

Chapter Four 21
The Third Pillar: Compassion

Chapter Five 25
The Fourth Pillar: Curiosity

Chapter Six 29
The Fifth Pillar: Humility

Chapter Seven 33
The Sixth Pillar: Patience

Chapter Eight 39
The Seventh Pillar: A Sense of Humor

Chapter Nine 45
The Eighth Pillar: Being a Mentor

Chapter Ten 49
Summary and Inspiration

Appendix 55

Index 57

Summary of Chapters

Introduction 1

Chapter One 3

> **Introduction to Zen.** This chapter explores the concept of Zen and ties it to fundraising and fundraisers. The eight pillars of success are introduced. The chapter concludes with a technique to settle and clear our minds.

Chapter Two 9

> **The First Pillar: Being in the Moment.** This pillar sets the stage for the remaining pillars. It is the foundation of Zen and mindfulness, which is the underlying theme of this book.

Chapter Three 15

> **The Second Pillar: Listening.** This pillar is especially critical for fundraisers because it opens the door to possibilities. It is also the key to forging successful relationships in fundraising as well as in life.

Chapter Four 21

> **The Third Pillar: Compassion.** Fundraisers often exercise their hearts, which flex and stretch as our donors share their stories, some sad and some uplifting. Donors transform their compassion into solutions through their gifts.

Chapter Five 25

> **The Fourth Pillar: Curiosity.** This pillar helps us engage with our donors, sparks our interest, and inspires us to ask "why?" Finding answers to this question is the essence of our jobs as fundraisers.

Chapter Six 29

The Fifth Pillar: Humility. This pillar is a key trait of some of the greatest figures in history. A humble person puts others at ease and creates a receptive environment. Humility is a characteristic of the most respected fundraisers.

Chapter Seven 33

The Sixth Pillar: Patience. If there were a golden rule of fundraising, it would be "Patience, patience, patience." Successful fundraisers learn that patience is the key to transformative gifts.

Chapter Eight 39

The Seventh Pillar: A Sense of Humor. Those who master this pillar can overcome almost any unexpected question, uncomfortable situation or difficult moment. This pillar enables us to have enjoyable moments—and careers—in fundraising.

Chapter Nine 45

The Eighth Pillar: Being a Mentor. Mentors inspire us even as they continue learning. The fortunate among us have had at least one great mentor. We then step up and serve as mentors.

Chapter Ten 49

Summary and Inspiration. This chapter summarizes the eight pillars and concludes with ten lessons I have learned from donors over almost two decades as a fundraiser.

Foreword

I can't believe it. If you know her, you won't either. Alexandra Pia Marie Brovey (AKA Alex) has gone completely off the rails! My best advice after reading this book? Go with her, or go alone. But go.

Alex is a charitable gift planner and fundraising professional of the highest caliber. She knows how to dance with charitable trusts, gift annuities, and retained life estates with the best of them. But, no, this book is not about tools and techniques, nor the strategies for solicitation—nothing that we usually consider as the stuff of fundraising.

Instead, Alex pauses to dwell on a deeply subjective journey she has undertaken from principle to practice, resting in that quiet place where practice itself is shaped and formed.

I'm so pleased to offer this foreword to Alex's journey of discovery. I find myself continually asking the question, why am I so drawn to Alex's story? In the fundraising field, especially at professional training conferences, we hear much about so-called transformational gifts. From my own and shared experiences, almost all of this is pure bunk—more talk about raising money for this season's campaign, then it's over and gone. For the most part, it is about deploying technical tools. Wasn't it Maslow who said, if you're a hammer, everything looks like a nail? But Alex writes about what to my mind is the real thing: the transformation of the institution; the transformation of the donor; and the most rarely spoken about, the transformation of the actual gift officer!

Alex introduces the eight pillars—touchstones of fundraising success that she discovered, and which guide her along the way. They are drawn from a separate, yet parallel, journey that led to her achieving a black belt in the martial art of karate. Alex grapples intensely with these twin disciplines—Zen and fundraising. She reinvents the so-called best practices of fundraising and goes much further than the technical fundraising gobbledygook we are immersed in daily.

And so, what you get here is a rare book that describes a place that not many fundraisers visit. (We just didn't know it was there!) You glimpse what happens in the mind and soul of the gift planner *before* the gift comes to life, even before it emerges from, well, wherever it comes from. And you can build a whole discipline and practice around that.

Alex rescues principles with the eight pillars that make the usual "fundraising tricks and secrets" seem trivial. The stuff that bombards us every day in what I have written about as the conventional fundraising matrix—all is ephemeral by comparison.

If you are a fundraiser, perhaps for the first time in your life you will think about what it *feels like* to do effective gift design. What will likely strike you about this is not the mere mechanics, but the underlying stuff of the calling. What it takes to become a good gift officer, or for that matter, a good *anything*.

In my own work on personalized philanthropy, I look for underlying principles and the impact that might follow from a shift away from the institutional perspective and toward the donor. The methods that emerged from that were like an awakening, more like a crashing which shook up my fundraising practice. Once you *see,* you have a new responsibility to *share.* Perhaps that's why Alex's book is not about the technical aspects of fundraising.

And perhaps, too, that is why Alex's work resonates so strongly with me. It might resonate with you as well. It's that place, I believe, where the phrase *joy of giving* has some meaning. That's joy in the sense of the Journey Outside Yourself. Anything less is, well ... just less.

Thinking expansively is nothing new for Alex. During her term as president of the Philanthropic Planning Group of Greater New York, it was my privilege to serve as a member of the board. During those years, the group became a kind of incubator of new leadership. For the past few years, I have had fun serving with Alex on the Leadership Institute of the National Association of Charitable Gift Planners, created to strengthen the bonds of veteran gift planners to the association formerly known as the National Committee on Planned Giving. For the next two years, Alex will serve as chair of the Leadership Institute and no doubt increase its ranks. Why? Because she is one of the people whom we want to be around.

So again, I'm asking: why has Alex has gone off the rails? Alex has amazing street cred as an estate attorney, gift officer, speaker, and contributor to the community of philanthropic advisors. She has become like the Zen archer who, becoming One with the target, hits the bullseye. From meditative practice and deep immersion, archer and target become indistinguishable and indivisible. That is a transformation few experience. For even the most sophisticated technical expert, striving is not enough. That's what Alex chose to write about.

You've heard of rails to trails? My best advice is to read this book and go off the rails a bit yourself. If you are a veteran gift officer, you'll find refreshment from realizing where your journey has taken you. If you are new to fundraising, from pillar to pillar you'll recognize the signposts on your path.

While the trail might not lead you, as it has Alex, to become a black belt in karate, it may at the very least inspire you to kick over a few conventions and achieve real fundraising mastery.

Steven L. Meyers, PhD
Author of *Personalized Philanthropy: Crash the Fundraising Matrix*

Introduction

Knowledge is learning something every day.

Wisdom is letting go of something each day.

Zen Proverb

This book is primarily for and about fundraisers. I hope that donors and advisors who work with fundraisers, and those who seek to find their Zen, will also find inspiration in this book. I define Zen and use it in this book to mean being centered and focused. Zen is not so much a destination as it is the moments along the journey.

I have devoted the bulk of my career to helping thousands of philanthropic people support the missions of four wonderful nonprofit organizations. I didn't plan to be a fundraiser, but looking back, the path (from law school, to an estate planning practice, to a volunteer for several nonprofits, to a job as a planned giving officer, to leading the gift planning team for a large metropolitan healthcare organization) is clear.

This book evolved in my mind over the years as I realized that a technical background is quite necessary for me, a gift planner. I have some familiarity with the Internal Revenue Code; I have drafted wills and charitable remainder trusts; I can explain tax law changes in understandable terms. However, the multitude of relationships I have been privileged to build with many generous donors is based on a far less technical but extremely critical set of skills. These are skills that fundraisers must possess to be successful. Further, they are also skills that embody successful people—in whatever their chosen careers—as well as in their personal relationships.

I earned my provisional black belt in Shotokan (traditional Japanese) karate in 2015. Earlier that year I began to meditate. The confluence of these two practices helped me to focus on several skills, which I call pillars, that are critical to success as a fundraiser. I sketched the outline for this book in the same way that I wrote many of my articles and presentations over the past dozen or so years: while commuting on the Long Island Rail Road!

As I began writing this book, my third Bernese Mountain Dog, Ferguson, would nudge me and bark when he wanted attention. He could be gentle or insistent, intermittent or pesky. After a while, I rewarded his efforts and patience by sitting on the sofa with ninety pounds of fur on my lap.

I contemplated the chapters on patience and curiosity, and something clicked: my dog (and his two predecessors, Napoleon and Leopold) exhibited some of the traits of excellent fundraisers! So, to lighten select chapters, I have included examples of how my dogs taught me to hone a pillar that I rely on in my role as a fundraiser, as well as in life.

Dogs seem to inherently live Zen lives. They live in the here and now. They do not appear to stress about tomorrow. They do not appear to relive yesterday. They enjoy the moment, and preferably the moments spent with their humans. Dog lovers will appreciate that I actually considered an alternate title: "What My Dog Taught Me About Fundraising…and Life!"

I wrote this book to impart useful information about how to be a more successful fundraiser. A side benefit is that these same skills lead to success in many other careers as well as in life.

Dear reader,

Sadly, after I wrote this book but prior to its publication, my beloved Ferguson died after eleven years of life. I miss him terribly, but know he lives on in the pages of this book and in my heart.

Chapter One

Introduction to Zen

> *We have two eyes to see two sides of things, but there must be a third eye which will see everything at the same time and yet not see anything. That is to understand Zen.*
>
> —D.T. Suzuki

Halfway through my career, I began to study martial arts, eventually earning a black belt in Shotokan karate. I have taken tai chi and Falun Dafa classes. I began to meditate; I visited a Buddhist monastery; and I practiced deep breathing in a salt cave. I read books about mindfulness and learned that a common way to focus while meditating is to count your breaths.

This led me to the discovery of the teachings of Thich Nhat Hahn, a Zen Master and author of numerous books focusing on mindfulness. He observed that if you were to draw a picture of the breath, it would look like a figure eight (my favorite number). It is interesting to note that an infinity sign is often described as a sleeping or a sideways figure eight.

Inspired by this Zen Master, I focused on the myriad of skills that are needed to be a great fundraiser. If someone were to create a multivitamin for fundraisers, what would be the essential ingredients? After much thought, I identified eight essential ingredients, which I call *pillars*, of fundraising success.

These pillars provide me immense strength and form a resilient support system to meet the unending challenges of an exciting and fulfilling fundraising career. They can do the same for you, too.

Here are the eight pillars:

- The First Pillar: Being in the Moment
- The Second Pillar: Listening
- The Third Pillar: Compassion
- The Fourth Pillar: Curiosity
- The Fifth Pillar: Humility
- The Sixth Pillar: Patience
- The Seventh Pillar: A Sense of Humor
- The Eighth Pillar: Being a Mentor

We'll dive into the pillars in the next chapters. But first…

Three Deep Breaths

A relaxed, alert state is optimal for performance. This applies to Olympic athletes, chess masters, business gurus, celebrity chefs, brain surgeons, parents… and fundraisers. Taking three deep breaths may assist you in maximizing the few moments before a meeting, a phone call, or a solicitation for a gift. Three deep breaths may enhance your mental alertness throughout a meeting, starting with the moments before it begins. Deep breathing enables you to be centered and focused.

Throughout this book I will occasionally suggest that you clear your mind by taking three deep breaths. While this is optional, I encourage you to try it this first time.

The next time you are preparing for a meeting or a phone call, take three deep breaths. (See sidebar on the next page.) Remind yourself that you bring all of your skills, knowledge, and memories with you to this moment. You bring your experiences to each interaction with your donors. You are the sum of all of your experiences.

Zen teaches us to focus on the present, the here and now. A beginner's mind wanders, back and forth and all around, reliving the past and anticipating the future and then reliving the past again. In this book we will focus on what makes us successful. We will build upon mistakes and lessons learned from the past, to ensure we have a successful future. But we will always return to the present moment.

Have you ever stopped to reflect on your first day or your first job as a fundraiser? Perhaps you replaced someone at a charity with a mature fundraising program. Possibly you were the first person hired to raise money at a young nonprofit. Maybe you were hired with a few others at the start of a capital campaign.

How did you feel on your first day? You may have felt a combination of excitement, pressure to succeed, pride in being hired, nervousness and optimism. Each time I started in a new position (as I write this book, I am working at my fourth nonprofit) I made a promise to raise more money, to work more collaboratively, and to do everything I could to achieve my goals. I'll let you know when I have finally succeeded.

The next time you arrive at work, take a moment to think about how you felt when you began versus how you feel today. Are you excited about the upcoming day? Are you reminiscing about the weekend? Are you bored,

---

How to Clear Your Mind

Sit in a quiet place. Begin to concentrate on your breath as it slows. Breathe naturally for about thirty seconds. Then take a deep breath and say to yourself, "Breathing in, I know I am breathing in." Exhale and say to yourself, "Breathing out, I know I am breathing out." Repeat two more times.

After taking three deep breaths, you will be calmer. Your heart rate will be slower. Your pulse will slow. (You can confirm that your pulse slows on a Fitbit, if you wear one.) Your mind will be clearer. Taking sixty seconds to do this will bring you to a more relaxed state.

Now that you have paused to "clear the slate" that was your busy mind, you will be better prepared to handle the next item on your agenda. For those who can recall chalkboards from elementary school, deep breathing for your mind is akin to cleaning a chalkboard so it is shiny and fresh for the next set of math formulas or sentence diagrams. Do this as often as you need to, and don't limit yourself to solicitation calls. Deep breathing has almost limitless applications. Try it when you are stuck in a traffic jam, sitting in a waiting room, or even before falling asleep, to clear your mind.

Practice makes perfect.

challenged or neutral about your work? Reflect on something you cherish about your job—perhaps your favorite coworker, donor or even flavor of coffee/tea! Consider getting a desk toy that makes you—and those who visit with you—smile and relax. I have an executive slinky, Art from Monsters University, and a baseball inscribed with the logo of the NYC subway system. A fingerprint expert would go ballistic if any of these are ever used in a crime.

Studies show that the act of smiling can elevate your mood and the mood of those around you, even when you are not happy. I enjoy helping others rediscover their smiles when they come into my office. When we then focus on the subject at hand, I believe we view it from a more positive starting point.

Your Most Meaningful Gift

Now take a few moments to recall some of the gifts you have raised throughout your career. Some gifts are especially rewarding because the ultimate use resonates with your values. (I am secretly grateful to donors when they make gifts that achieve some of my personal goals.) Perhaps you received a gift at a critical time that helped you to achieve your annual goals. No doubt you can recall your largest gift.

Now I challenge you to recall your *most meaningful gift*. If you wish, take a moment to close your eyes and think about it. This gift is one you would share with someone new to fundraising when asked why you chose this career, or with a respected colleague after a day at a conference, or perhaps recall after you retire. (Save the story about the largest gift for your next job interview.) When you ponder your most meaningful gift, you may discover that what you really treasure about this gift is the impact of the gift and its meaning to the donor, more than the amount of the gift or even the ultimate (unknown) beneficiaries.

I have asked several gift planning colleagues, "What is your most meaningful gift?" Not once was the most meaningful gift the largest one. I am not surprised. I wonder if the answer would be the same if the question were posed to *donors* who have made multiple gifts to one or more nonprofits. Would they select the largest gift as their most meaningful?

I have personally solicited and received gifts from hundreds of generous people. The size of the gifts ranged from a few pennies to more than $12 million, and many amounts in between. These gifts came from people both young and old, wealthy and modest, and were large and small, current and deferred.

My most meaningful gift was made by a mother who divided her modest estate into shares equal to the number of her sons—five—plus one. The sixth share is slated for the university which provided her with a scholarship. I had a chance to meet with this mother in person to discuss her intended gift over breakfast before she went to work. She had tears in her eyes as she shared with me that she had waited her whole life (over sixty years) to be able to give back and express her appreciation. My recollection of the gift amount is $25,000. At many nonprofits this amount is no longer considered a "major" gift. But to this donor it was a most generous tribute to what her university education meant to her.

Do Fundraising and Zen Go Together?

The title of this book, *Zen and the Art of Fundraising*, pairs two themes—Zen and fundraising. I can just hear the critics (including many fundraisers) responding: Fundraising is stressful. We constantly must surpass last year's goal. Our donors say "no," our bosses say "more," and changing tax laws and revolving colleagues are a constant. Fundraising is *not* Zen. It is the antithesis of Zen. These two concepts can never coexist.

Or can they?

Zen is broadly defined as "a state of centeredness which is here and now… a concentration of mind." When we focus our attention primarily on the donor and the donor's goals, and pair that with our nonprofit's needs and priorities, we fall within the meaning of the definition. The pursuit of "donor-focused fundraising" requires concentrating on the donor's needs and goals. I believe fundraising can be Zen, and we can find Zen here as well as in many other areas of life.

As the quote at the beginning of this chapter intimated, we sometimes need to go beyond what is obvious from the donor's view or the fundraiser's view to get to the "third eye." The ultimate result might not be known at the outset, but it will be unveiled (like a masterpiece) as you and your donors work together toward a gift.

When I began as a planned giving officer almost two decades ago—I now call myself a charitable gift planner—I was proud of my skill set as an estate planning attorney. I had earned additional degrees and gained knowledge of gift techniques and the tax benefits of a variety of gift options. As the years passed, however, it became obvious to me that donors *first and subsequently* judge fundraisers by certain skills. These can be as simple as how we answer the phone during an initial call, whether we truly listen to their needs and goals, our ability to engage in a conversation about a wide variety of topics, and how and whether we are responsive to the donors' needs.

When I am routinely asked what makes a fundraiser successful, my response has traditionally been that successful fundraisers possess a combination of skills, both "hard" and "soft." This book focuses on and describes the soft, non-technical skills.

In this book, we will apply mindfulness and Zen concepts to our roles as fundraisers. The result, I hope, will be to emerge not only as better fundraisers but also as calmer persons. While donors will continue to give to achieve their goals, it should not be surprising that they do so with more joy—and perhaps in greater amounts—with fundraisers who master the eight pillars of success.

> *Wherever you go, there you are.*
>
> —Traditional Zen Proverb

Chapter Two

The First Pillar: Being in the Moment

> *We do not remember days, we remember moments.*
>
> —Cesare Pavese

Some moments with donors are forever imprinted on our minds. I visited with donors in the greater Washington, DC area on September 11, 2001, when the terrorists struck. My first visit was with a couple who lived north of Silver Spring, Maryland. We had previously spoken on the phone, and they had requested illustrations for a six-figure charitable gift annuity. My goals were to discuss their interest in an annuity, respond to any questions, and hopefully leave with their promise to make a gift.

I can close my eyes and recall the scene as if it were last week: I knocked on their door, greeted them in person for the first time, and asked if they would mind turning on the television. (I have never done this before or since. How rude this seems out of context—but that day was an aberration.) They turned on the television, sat down on either side of me on a three-cushion sofa, and we held hands as the towers fell. I quickly revised my goals as we sat together in silence. A six-figure gift suddenly seemed insignificant in light of world terrorism. I met with two other couples that day, and a few more over the next two days. Our conversations were less focused on gifts and more focused on life and death, war and peace.

Donors share some of their most memorable lifetime moments with us. And sometimes—like on September 11—we involuntarily share moments. A few of these may actually become our own memorable moments. After almost two decades, I am still touched deeply when donors share their hopes and dreams, hugs and thanks for assisting them in achieving some lifetime goals. Donors' gifts and kindness echo and reverberate across time.

Fundraisers have a front-row seat to our donors' happiest moments and most troubling hardships. Our donors assist in eradicating some of the miseries of the world (hunger, sickness, illiteracy, homelessness, lost souls). They invite us into their worlds to assist them, and we get to experience their wonder, joy, and happiness. This job is not for the meek! Being in the moment takes courage.

Take a few minutes to recall some key moments with your donors. Are any of them imprinted on your mind? Was the occasion a happy one? A sad one? Or perhaps it was the totality of a day. I recall one day which began with an educational session, followed by a meeting with an advisor to collect a large check, and ending with a shiva for the ninety-plus-year-old spouse of one of my donors. The day was one of intellectual stimulation, excitement, and sadness.

The Path to a Gift

The essence of a fundraiser's job is determining why someone wishes to give, matching those intentions to the nonprofit's goals, helping the donor structure the gift, accepting the gift, and then thanking the donor for the gift, both in word and in deed.

Sounds easy, right?

This process is a journey, a "path to a gift" which requires spending time with donors to discover what motivates them. Some of us find it easy to carry on a conversation. We can keep it going, mostly with our own comments, opinions, and observations. While some prospective donors would love to know more about us, this is not the purpose of the meeting. We have to train ourselves to really focus on the donor. We have to learn to be in the moment for the precious few minutes we are together.

All of the latest research and strategy sessions cannot replace information shared directly by the donor. This is a magical exchange! During meetings, we give the donor the important gifts of time and our attention. Donors, in turn, give us the gifts of their time, access to their reasons for giving, and ultimately their gifts.

The Zen concept of *being in the moment* can inspire us in assessment, cultivation, and solicitation meetings. Mindfulness seeks to calm life down to this moment. We recognize there is a past, and that there will be a future. But we need to learn to focus on right here, right now. We can apply this concept to our fundraising jobs in several ways.

> **Try This**
>
> The next time you speak with a donor, take a few moments after you hang up to write down some notes. Continue to reflect on the call. Spend a few moments simply appreciating the relationship with this donor. After all, this is the essence of our jobs. Review your notes prior to your next contact to reacquaint yourself with this donor.

First, when speaking or meeting with donors, we should put aside all extraneous thoughts and simply be in the moment. Actual moments with donors likely do not exceed 10 to 20 percent of our time—but we should give them 110 percent of our attention.

Second, when we practice being in the moment, our attention shifts from extraneous thoughts to what—who—is in front of us: *the donor.*

> *The most precious gift we can offer anyone is our attention.*
>
> Thich Nhat Hanh

Third, when you are truly in the moment with your donors, you will be able to enjoy the time developing the relationship and relax. A relaxed state might enable you to make a connection you hadn't thought of before. Such moments are special and are echoes of the joy and goodness that philanthropy embodies.

Plot Your Donor's Journey

The path to a gift is in many ways analogous to the plot we learned about in middle school English class. You may recall that plot is defined as events that make up a story or the main part of a story. [Literarydevices.net] Plot generally has five elements: introduction, rising action, climax, falling action, and epilogue. A typical donor cycle also has five elements: discovery, cultivation, solicitation, closure, and stewardship. I overlaid the elements from a typical donor cycle onto a plot diagram, to plot a typical donor's journey.

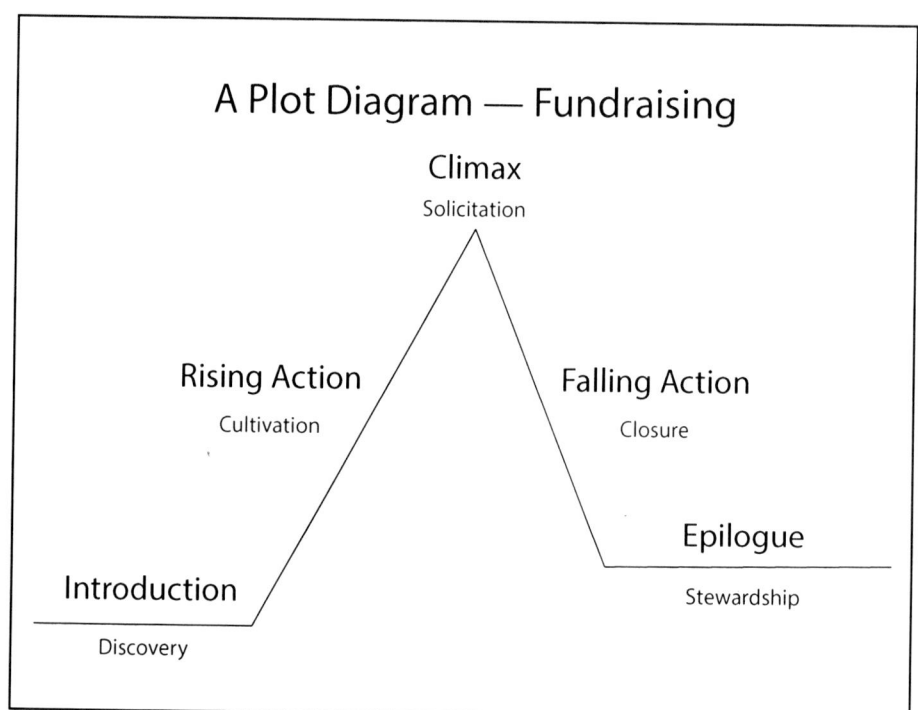

Introduction—Discovery

The *introduction* presents the characters and sets the scene. In a gift scenario, this is the discovery phase during which you gather information about your prospective donor. For example, you may get a phone call from a donor who shares that she is a school teacher, is single, and doesn't have children. She has taught for thirty years, and cares deeply about children and their health. She is the caregiver for her elderly mother.

Rising Action—Cultivation

The *rising action* is a series of events that builds up to the conflict. In the gift scenario, the cultivation phase involves getting to know the donor and discovering what inspires the donor, so that you begin to focus on a gift solicitation. You may meet with the school teacher and take her on a tour of the children's hospital. At some point she shares that she is planning to retire. A few months later, her mother passes away. Both events bring emotional and financial changes for the school teacher. She is likely to have more available time, and perhaps she focuses on her own mortality. She calls to share that she would like to make a gift to help children. She would also like to honor her late mother. She has engaged an estate planning attorney. She may also be interested in volunteering.

Climax—Solicitation

The *climax* is a turning point. In our gift scenario, the school teacher transforms into a donor. She responds positively to a solicitation (which was previously vetted by her and shared with her in draft form) and establishes a fund that bears her mother's name and will make perpetual distributions to help children with neurological issues. The donor is pleased and your nonprofit will provide medical care to additional children. A win-win scenario for everyone.

Falling Action—Closure

The *falling action* includes events that wind down the plot. In our gift scenario, the donor may have to complete some paperwork. The medical team caring for children can express gratitude and share with the donor the impact of her gift. The fundraiser and others who collaborated on this gift (perhaps some of the children and their parents) can send thank-you notes. The donor may agree to be profiled so her philanthropic journey can be memorialized, shared, and celebrated.

Epilogue—Stewardship

The *epilogue* is the end of the story. In the gift scenario, the receipt of the gift is both an end (to a solicitation) and a beginning. Like a commencement, this moment is the start of the post-gift, stewardship phase of the journey. The philanthropy seed which began with an idea and resulted in a gift now transforms for the benefit of humanity.

Use Some Kindergarten Strategies

Does your average day and attention to tasks resemble a kindergarten class at recess? Do you feel like you are running in ten different directions and need to play on every piece of apparatus before the bell rings? Perhaps we should borrow a command from kindergarten teachers to "freeze!" Alternatively, a "time out"—even a self-imposed one—can help us focus our attention on this particular moment. Are the steps we are taking right now leading us in the right direction?

When my dog Ferguson nudges me, I am often in the middle of an activity. But he has a knack for redirecting my attention to the present moment and—more specifically—to him. He is most certainly enjoying the "now" when I pet him, and I take a few moments to enjoy being with him. Pet owners are fortunate to get an occasional nudge to savor the moment. When we are away from our pets, we can continue the practice of being in the moment.

Fundraisers work with multiple donors—perhaps numbering in the hundreds—at any given time. We help donors throughout all the stages of giving. Sometimes when we are preparing to ask someone for money, a donor who has already made a gift calls and we need to redirect our attention for a short while. And then a prospective donor calls to begin a gift conversation. We continually need to rebalance and prioritize. Being in the moment with each donor enables us to maximize our time efficiently.

Anytime you feel you have strayed from the present moment or need to refocus, pause and take three deep breaths. Look inward. Usually, change has to happen within our own minds first.

> *Life is a dance.*
>
> *Mindfulness is*
>
> *witnessing that dance.*
>
> —Amit Ray

Chapter Three

The Second Pillar: Listening

> *He who does not understand your silence*
>
> *will probably not understand your words.*
>
> —Elbert Hubbard

I dedicated one Sunday to experience a "Day of Mindfulness" at the Blue Cliff Monastery in Pine Bush, NY, approximately two hours north of New York City. Much of my six-hour stay included silence and meditation. A one-hour group meditative walk in the woods was done in silence (enabling us to hear a bird tweeting and a bullfrog croaking). Deer peeked at us as we entered the big meditation hall. We listened to a talk by one of the Buddhist monks, and shared reflections. Afterward, we sat together and ate a vegan meal in silence. We left with peaceful hearts.

Silence is easier to find in the middle of the mountains. However, external silence can make the internal noise—the critic in our heads—seem that much louder. Silence can actually be quite loud. We sometimes speak to try to cancel out noise, either external or internal. Multitaskers beware: speaking and listening are mutually exclusive. These two activities *cannot* be accomplished at the same time.

To be successful, we need to discover what motivates our donors. We need to learn to quiet our voices and our minds, and listen. In fact, we need to do much more listening than speaking throughout most of our donor interactions. A good rule to remember is to refrain from speaking until you spend some time listening. One suggestion for quieting your mind is to count to yourself. As we learned in Chapter One, you can begin by counting your breaths.

On his eightieth birthday, Zen Master Thich Nhat Hanh was asked whether he plans to retire as a teacher. He responded, "Teaching is done not only by talking, but also by living your own life… You don't need to talk in order to teach. You need to live your life mindfully and deeply."

It is human nature to talk and to fill a void with words. Perhaps we can learn from our older donors, some of whom take more time to pull together their thoughts. They are not in such a hurry to speak. When we are among older people we slow from our faster (default) speed. This gives us time to let our words catch up to our thoughts. We do not need to fill all of those silent moments.

By practicing receptive listening when others are speaking, we can create a receptive environment. This can be difficult for those trained as attorneys who solicit information by asking questions, so that they can tailor the advice. In *The 7 Habits of Highly Effective People: Powerful Lessons in Personal Change,* Stephen R. Covey said it best: "Most people do not listen with the intent to understand; they listen with the intent to reply."

Listening is an underrated skill. When we listen, we hope to hear our donors' goals and wishes, information about their families and careers, and the reasons they are inspired to make a gift. Listening helps us to respond more thoughtfully. We can reflect and then use the information to help craft gifts that assist our donors in achieving their goals.

A Recipe for Listening

Listening requires quieting your voice and your mind. A useful recipe for honing this key pillar is this:

> Listen.
>
> Reflect.
>
> Respond.
>
> Repeat!

What a simple recipe—it only has four ingredients. (If only tonight's dinner were as simple.)

Listening has been identified as an important skill in a number of venues and throughout time. In the Bible, the book of Ecclesiastes states that there is a time to be quiet and a time to speak. Presumably, during the quiet time, one is expected to listen.

A sweet children's rhyme—The Wise Old Owl—reinforces the importance of listening.

> *The Wise Old Owl sat on an oak.*
>
> *The more he saw, the less he spoke.*
>
> *The less he spoke, the more he heard.*
>
> *Why can't we all be like that wise old bird?*
>
> —Author Unknown

As the poem illustrates, when you allow your other senses to do their jobs, you will actually hear (listen) more. When you reflect on a conversation or a meeting with a donor, you will be better able to recall nuances of the conversation, even those parts not shared in words, if you have spent some quality time listening.

Just as medicine is personalized, so should philanthropy be personalized to each donor. Steven L. Meyers, PhD, in his book *Personalized Philanthropy: Crash the Fundraising Matrix,* shared the mantra, "The right gift, for the right donor, for the right purpose, at the right time." Knowing when you have it *right* is only achievable if you know your donor's goals. And that is only possible when you listen.

Some years ago, Barbara R. Diehl, Esq., who was then the Manager of Gift Planning for the American Red Cross in New York, presented "What Did You Say? Listening Your Way to a Planned Gift" to the then Planned Giving Group of Greater New York. A few points in that presentation still resonate.

First, listening is not passive, it is active. This means your brain is actively working. Listening requires a good amount of energy.

I recall my early years in gift planning when I traveled to another part of the country to visit with three, four, or even five individuals or couples in one day. By the time I arrived at my hotel late in the day, my face felt frozen, and I could barely muster the energy to get to my room. My brain was "on" for much of the day, focused on remembering key information about each person, including children and pet names, areas of interest, preliminary gift ideas, and more. We don't often think of brain work as tiring, or as tiring as physical exercise. But it most certainly is. And it's energy well spent.

Second, the listener sets the direction of the conversation. Many operate under the misconception that the speaker sets the direction. But the speaker usually only continues for as long as the speaker receives feedback from the listener. Since we can hear and comprehend far faster than a person can speak, we need time to process what a speaker is saying.

Some of us need more practice listening and less practice speaking. I am referring specifically to those who love to speak, can carry a conversation, and who might walk out of a four-hour meeting with less-than-optimal results because they spent the majority of the time speaking. While it's hard to truly and unemotionally observe yourself, for your own success ask a friend (as I did) if you need to work harder at being a good listener. True friends tell the truth, and this might be one skill that you can hone to achieve success.

> **The speaker only continues for as long as the speaker receives feedback from the listener.**

Meetings with Multiple People

Your ability to listen might be affected—positively or negatively—by those present. Meetings can take place one-on-one, or with multiple fundraisers, donors, or advisors.

Some meetings might be more successful when colleagues accompany each other on donor visits. Together you may recall much more of the conversation, and each person brings unique skills and insights to the meeting. Other meetings might not be as successful, such as when a oursome (two fundraisers and two donors) breaks into two couples, and the conversation becomes fragmented.

I recall visiting with a couple in southern California who liked to finish each other's sentences. If I posed a question to the wife, the husband answered, and vice versa. I guess thirty-plus years of marriage bestows a certain familiarity. I spent the least amount of time talking, and ironically, they started posing questions to each other that I otherwise would have asked. "Don—wasn't that meteorologist on television your best professor?" It was almost like watching a television sit-com. And I had a front-row seat.

Another couple is so aligned that they both participate in every phone call, each from an extension. I was surprised the first time, after I had been speaking with one spouse for about ten minutes, when the other piped in with some additional information. Now I look forward to these calls. And I have the added benefit of not having to wonder what the spouse thinks. This is a concern when I am speaking about a legacy gift and I have only had the opportunity to speak with one spouse. It's important to know what the donor's spouse thinks. The donor's spouse could be the survivor and could modify your donor's original plans to make a gift.

One interpretation of the quote at the beginning of the chapter is that your silence is a sign that you respect others and want to hear their thoughts. Listening is a compliment to the speaker. Being a good listener makes you an easy person to converse with. And this will deepen your relationships with donors. Also, allowing others to speak will often mean that when it is your turn to speak, you will be given the same respect. Strong relationships are built upon mutual respect. And the foundation is simple: be a good listener.

The word 'listen' contains the same letters

as the word 'silent.'

—Alfred Brendel

Chapter Four

The Third Pillar: Compassion

> *Yesterday I was clever, so I wanted to change the world.*
>
> *Today I am wise, so I am changing myself.*
>
> —Rumi

Early in my career I scheduled a full day of visits with donors about three hours away from my home. I didn't know it at the time, but I had torn my anterior cruciate ligament (ACL) and medial meniscus playing tennis the previous evening. Not allowing this "minor" setback to keep me from visiting my donors, I started on my trip.

By lunchtime I had traveled over 150 miles and visited two households. In the first home, the donor insisted I elevate my leg on her sofa. In the second home, a couple gave me an ice pack that the wife had used after her knee surgery. By the time I hobbled from my car into the reception area of a retirement community to visit a couple for lunch, I was in pain. The donors—a lively couple in their eighties—introduced themselves to me, took one look at my face, and moved into action.

The husband latched onto my left arm, the wife onto my right arm, and together they escorted me (barely thirty years old) up the handicapped ramp into the dining room! In addition to a good lunch, I ate a hefty serving of humble pie for dessert. (In **Chapter Six,** we will explore the pillar of humility.)

Many of the prospects and donors whom I have had the pleasure of meeting are in their sixties, seventies, and eighties, and have had their knees replaced. Up to this point I listened to numerous stories about their pain, doctors' appointments, surgeries and rehabilitation afterward, and difficulties moving around. I sympathized with them. Now that I have experienced knee surgery and physical therapy myself—*having limped the same path*—I can empathize and better relate to this segment of the donor population. Understanding others' suffering builds compassion.

Pairing Pillars

Compassion is defined as a feeling of deep sympathy and sorrow for another who is stricken by misfortune, accompanied by a strong desire to alleviate the suffering.

Compassion is a key element in several of the world's major religions. It is one of the precepts of Buddhism and is a key trait to attain the state of enlightenment. It is also one of the three end goals of Chinese Falun Gong. In the Bible, 1 Peter states: *Finally, all of you, live in harmony with one another; be sympathetic, love as brothers, be compassionate and humble.*

Compassion is a pillar that pairs well with being a good listener, the previous pillar. I think of compassion as empathy-plus. You show you care by listening to the donor and acknowledging your donors' feelings.

Particularly in healthcare fundraising, we hear many stories, some tragic. The death of a child, a parent who no longer recognizes a child, the long road to recovery after losing a limb—all require a high level of compassion, the highest level you can muster without having experienced these situations yourself. Some of these moments present a good opportunity to take three deep breaths and reset.

I personally balance the sad stories with the happy ones: the birth of a child who was conceived through in vitro fertilization; open-heart surgery that saves a parent; a spouse's hip surgery that enables the couple to dance on their fiftieth wedding anniversary. Zen recognizes—and teaches us to accept—the cycles of ups and downs in the universe. One way to acknowledge this cycle is to refocus our attention on the positive moments: life-saving research and technology, skilled surgeons, loving care from nurses, a new graduating class of highly trained and compassionate doctors.

Whatever type of nonprofit you work for, be as compassionate as you can. When you are called upon to assist your donors through difficult moments, practice your pillar of being a good listener. Even if you can do nothing to fix the problem, simply listening may provide comfort to the donor.

Later, you can counter the difficult moments by quietly reflecting on your organization's successes. Smile as three puppies are rescued; or ten scholarships are awarded; or an art therapy program is introduced at a senior center; or five trees are planted; or meals are prepared for 150 homeless families.

Sync or Sink

One critical step in the process is connecting—or syncing—with your donors. Wouldn't it be great if there were a plug that we could connect from our donors to our laptops? We could download their true goals, reservations, fears, and hopes. Caution is needed, however, as these connections often flow both ways. So before syncing, consider your own true motives, hopes, and fears, and the possibility that your donors might be able to see those. Will they like what they see?

While you are striving to sync with your donors, you can practice your skills by syncing with your colleagues. When you are part of a team, take the time to imagine yourself in your colleague's shoes in the moments before or after a meeting and when you are discussing a particular donor or gift scenario. What do your colleagues want or need to accomplish, and how can you assist them?

Strategy sessions can help uncover everyone's goals and objectives, and set the course of action. Even while you are pursuing your own goals—which hopefully align with your colleague's goals—keep in mind the overarching purpose of the meeting. Keep the focus ultimately where it belongs: on the donor. What does the donor wish to accomplish?

If your annual goals or closing the gift should ever become more important than the donor and the donor's goals, you need to take some time out to reconnect with your Zen. As the quote at the start of this chapter teaches, work on changing yourself first. Only then can you best assist your donors.

Compassionate Donors Change the World

We can learn lessons daily from our donors, whose compassion flows in the form of gifts. Cancer survivors are one special category of donors who are keen on alleviating others' suffering. Survivors' groups have formed, both to celebrate life and to provide strength to current cancer patients. Parents who have lost children are another special category of donors. Their compassion enables them to support a stranger who unfortunately is no stranger to the unique suffering of these parents.

Most gifts are gifts of money or other assets that can be reduced to cash. Perhaps the ultimate act of compassion is to donate an organ (such as a kidney) or to consent to the donation of a loved one's organs after an untimely death. Not only are these stories deservedly the occasional high points of the nightly news, but these acts of compassion directly save or improve many lives.

> *No act of kindness,*
>
> *no matter how small,*
>
> *is ever wasted.*
>
> —Aesop

Personal Dedication

I am very grateful to the anonymous and kind human being who donated the ACL adopted by my right knee which I have called my own for the past fifteen years. I realize I can never repay this donor. I can only follow my donor's unselfish example and express my intent to be an organ donor myself. I dedicate this chapter to my donor. *Thank you.*

Chapter Five

The Fourth Pillar: Curiosity

> *Maybe you are searching among the branches*
>
> *for what only appears in the roots.*
>
> —Rumi

Great fundraisers focus on the missions of their nonprofit organizations. But more is needed to be an excellent fundraiser. You must also focus on the missions of your donors. This is what we learned to listen for in Chapter Three. This exploration—driven by our curiosity—will guide our donors and us on the path toward a gift. One that will fulfill both donors' and nonprofits' missions.

Curiosity is defined as a desire to know or inquisitive interest in others' concerns. My contemporaries and I learned about curiosity from a cartoon monkey, Curious George. Curiosity led George on some interesting adventures. Thankfully our human brains keep us out of most of George's troubles, the occasional side effects of curiosity.

Curious people occupy a prime place in the history books. Albert Einstein and Leonardo da Vinci possessed heaps of curiosity. According to *Time,* Da Vinci had notebooks filled with pages of questions, such as what caused people to yawn, methods to square a circle, what makes an aortic valve close, and how to describe the tongue of a woodpecker. Curious people often ask "why?" Asking this question too often and at a young age was likely viewed as "cheeky." We might have been in trouble for asking too many questions. Don't let that stop you now.

Curiosity is a positive trait, and a pillar, for fundraisers. Asking "why?" is one of the best questions to pose to a prospective donor at a first meeting. But don't stop asking. Successful fundraisers continue to ask "why?" at other times. When your donor makes a bigger gift, ask "why?" When your donor makes a gift for a new purpose, ask "why?" When your donor considers including a gift through an estate plan, ask "why?"

Also ask "why?" in the inverse situations. When your donor doesn't attend an event, ask "why?" When your donor doesn't make a gift, ask "why?" When your donor reduces the amount of the gift from prior years, ask "why?" In some cases, the answers are not a cause for alarm. Perhaps the donor was otherwise occupied, alternates gifts among charities, or experienced a hardship.

Relationships are not built entirely on happy moments. Some relationships with donors begin when the donor identifies a problem or expresses dissatisfaction. Although you might not succeed in finding a patient's missing clothes, you can correct a misspelled name, and you can listen when someone expresses frustration with the services provided by your nonprofit. If your donor is willing to share these concerns and issues, and you provide a listening ear, you will be a more effective ambassador for your nonprofit. And the donor may make a gift.

Questions that curious fundraisers ask their donors include: Why are you interested in funding [this cause]? Why now? Why did you choose to use stock to make a gift? Curious fundraisers ask with a genuine focus on what drives each donor. The "intel" donors provide enable us to be more effective in assisting them in discovering the best assets, over the best time frame, which will achieve the donors' goals.

A mentor of mine once observed, "You take your donors as you find them." In Zen terms, *It is as it is.* Our donors are not who we wish they were, they are who they are. We should always be focused on finding ways to meet them where they are and to help them achieve their goals.

Some donors do not clearly state why they want to make a gift. Instead, they share that they are not motivated by having their names on a wall. They do not seek a tax deduction. They do not want to allocate their gift proceeds to a particular purpose. And they don't want to waste your time and meet with you for lunch. (So much for that meeting metric.)

Instead of labeling these donors, simply accept them. Continue to listen. Keep asking questions. Sometimes the best way to the center of a maze is to cross off the paths that lead nowhere. What remains is the path to where you want to be.

Uncovering Goals

Imagine that you need a new computer. You go to a store with a particular model in mind. A good salesperson doesn't lead you directly to that model but instead asks what you plan to use it for, and then leads you to (usually) a higher functioning and more expensive model that can do more than you thought you needed—plus an extended warranty! Even those of us who are cost-conscious and did some research can be persuaded to purchase the better model. And we are pleased with the purchase.

The same concept applies to giving. The goal is to ask why and listen to the response. Then you can assist prospective donors in discovering the best gift options. In the optimum circumstances, the donor will make the largest gift possible, especially if you are able to introduce concepts such as a *blended gift* or a *legacy gift*. Donors may not be aware of all the ways charitable giving can achieve multiple goals. It is our job, our duty, to educate and share opportunities with them—for their own benefit as well as the benefit of humankind.

Fundraisers in younger generations like to play games on the latest iPhone apps. Delving into your donors' needs and desires over time is like winning the lower levels of a game and uncovering exciting new levels in a game app. Both fundraisers and gamers share that great feeling when achieving

---

What is a "blended" gift?

Although there are a number of possible definitions, I define a blended gift as a gift comprised of multiple parts—usually a gift now plus, often in the donor's will, a gift later. One benefit of a blended gift is that the donor can see the impact immediately, getting an appetizer-size taste of the ultimate and larger impact of the donor's gift that will be received at a later time.

What is a "legacy" gift?

I define a "legacy gift" as a gift that may begin during life but which is enhanced or completed at death, usually as part of an estate plan. Some equate a legacy gift with an endowed gift that bears the donor's name and provides funds in perpetuity.

a higher level. I can almost see the fireworks exploding when I make a breakthrough with a donor. For example, when a donor I have spoken with and exchanged emails with for eight years (yes, really!) calls me and says "The time is right—I am ready," I am thrilled. One hundred bonus points and on to the next level!

Trees and Roots

We began the chapter with a quote about trees and roots. Did you know that as glorious as being surrounded by trees in a forest truly is, we only see the one-third of the tree that is above ground? The other two-thirds of the tree is below ground. That is where the roots live.

A recent walk through the woods looking at (partial) trees made me think about how much—or how little—of our donors' goals and objectives we actually know. Can we call our interactions a "relationship" when we know one-third of what we need to know? As the relationship grows deeper, we may "dig" and uncover another one-third. Over time—a few years, a few decades?—we can strive to discover the remaining one-third.

Our ultimate goal is to nurture our relationships with donors to the point where we can together explore their roots—literally and figuratively. What we can expect to discover in the roots are the original motivations for gifts, childhood and early experiences that sprouted the seeds of philanthropy, and all of the donors' big and little experiences that bring them to this moment when we are focusing together on their gift intentions. We just need to keep asking "why?"

My Bernese Mountain Dog, Ferguson—like Curious George mentioned at the beginning of this chapter—has a high level of curiosity. He isn't hesitant to bark at the first knock, to approach just about anyone on the street, and to sniff every person and item. If we as fundraisers can adopt some of this curiosity, it will help us ask "why" more often. Asking "why" helps us get answers to questions that get to the roots and deepen our relationships.

Just ask why.

> *The important thing is not to stop questioning.*
>
> *Curiosity has its own reason for existing.*
>
> —Albert Einstein

Chapter Six

The Fifth Pillar: Humility

> *Life is a long lesson in humility.*
>
> —James M. Barrie

In **Chapter Four**, I shared the story of being escorted to lunch in an assisted living facility by an eighty-year-old couple. This is the opposite of the usual scenario, considering the fifty-year difference in our ages at the time. This story remains one of my most memorable ones some fifteen years later. I occasionally think about that couple and wonder whether they are still alive. How many laughs did they enjoy over the years about escorting someone the age of their grandchildren to lunch?

This "escort service" taught me about the importance of being humble. I might have been a bit mortified at the time, although pain has a way of preempting other worries. It's not easy asking for or accepting help. The same is true of asking for money.

Most fundraisers did not intend to make fundraising a career, nor did they earn a degree in fundraising. Most began careers as lawyers, financial planners, in marketing or sales, or in a variety of other areas—even as musicians or chaplains.

Those of us who transitioned from practicing law were (notwithstanding myriad jokes) once held in high esteem. We likely eat a piece of humble pie at cocktail parties. "So, you're an attorney. What type of law do you practice?" The answer "I am a fundraiser" usually does not inspire backslaps and nods. (A fresh drink or the restroom seem to beckon on these occasions.)

Many people equate fundraisers with civil servants. Someone has to do the job (and thank goodness it's not me). If we take a broad view of a fundraiser's role, it is not simply to ask for money. Rather, we are asking someone if they would like to fulfill a childhood promise. Or help someone overcome a hardship. Or make life better for a stranger. Or fulfill a moral or religious need to give. Or reap other tangible or intangible benefits. The real question we ask is, "Will you help?" A gift—money—is but a means to an end.

Humility Opens the Door to Opportunity

Humility is freedom from pride and arrogance.

Humility shapes our characters and makes us better fundraisers. A humble person views every situation as an opportunity, and as a chance to do better. Being humble usually puts people around you at ease. While much of society is in an unwritten competition, many donors—especially those focused on including a charity in their wills—are more focused on making a difference. Some even do so anonymously.

Humility is required to accept scholarship support, or temporary housing, or food from a food bank. Appreciation for others' generosity can and does inspire giving at a future date when personal circumstances change.

I had the pleasure of speaking with a donor who had received scholarship support forty years ago when she was a student. When she won the lottery (not the big one, but big enough!), she decided to "pay back" the scholarship. Being in a position to make a dream come true in the form of a charitable gift transforms humility into pride. And probably a level of pride that someone who did not have to accept scholarship support cannot come close to matching.

Humility Inspires Greatness

In the school-age Magic Tree House series by Mary Pope Osborne, books 49 to 52 feature young siblings Jack and Annie who are on a quest to discover the four secrets of greatness. They learn that the first secret of greatness is humility. (Incidentally, the other three are hard work, meaning and purpose, and enthusiasm.) Alexander the Great, and some of the greatest figures in history, were humble.

Isn't it interesting that those who have achieved so much, who should rightfully be so proud of their accomplishments, are usually the ones who defer to others' thoughts and ideas? They redirect attention away from

themselves. Some familiar examples of humble (and great) persons include Jesus, the Buddha, Gandhi, Sister Teresa, George Washington, and Jackie Robinson. Who else comes to mind?

Some of the donors you will meet come from very humble backgrounds. They were the first persons in their families to attend college. They may have come to the United States with less than two hundred dollars in their pockets. They understand the value of hard work, they remember those who gave them a chance, and they have a glowing ember within them that inspires them to give back when they are able to do so. You are a fortunate fundraiser when you find these gems and discover and nurture their connections to your nonprofit.

Some who hold the highest positions in companies have worked in a variety of entry, low-paying jobs earlier in their careers. I had the privilege (and the burden) of going to a donor's apartment shortly after he had passed away. I was not alone—the nonprofit's attorney and financial officer were also present. The apartment and its contents were donated to the nonprofit through the donor's estate. Our role was to inventory the contents. After a few hours, we took a lunch break, and spent most of the time trading stories about the worst jobs we had ever held, each story trying to top the last one. Three people holding the highest titles in their respective units had held summer jobs including shop sweeper, golf caddy, fast food worker, and newspaper delivery person. We laughed and noted what a long way we had come. The lessons we learned from those early jobs—being on time, having pride in our work, being respectful, appreciating the (little) money we earned—built our characters and formed a foundation for future success.

Arrogance is the opposite of humility. I have not met many arrogant fundraisers. We self-select, and it's not in a fundraiser's DNA to be arrogant. Arrogance interferes with teamwork. Arrogance can be a turn-off to donors who like to (and deserve to) feel appreciated for making a gift.

The vast majority of donors lack arrogance. They can and should be proud of being in a position to make a gift. Every once in a rare while, a fundraiser will have to interact with an arrogant donor. One donor commented to me about being able to "buy anything I want, including time with you." Right. I have been lucky to (humbly) hold in my hands a few gift checks that exceeded my annual salary. Some colleagues report to a boss who is in a younger generation. These moments present a good opportunity to take three deep breaths and reset. These moments also present you with opportunities to hone the pillar of humility.

I have met a few humble millionaires. They enjoy having lunch at diners, driving modest cars, and spending free time in their gardens, quilting, or fishing. Some wish to make anonymous gifts, declining the opportunity to have their names publicized. You can read more about a subcategory of millionaires in *The Millionaire Next Door*. As one millionaire-donor shared, she feels fortunate and only knows how to live a humble life.

You can practice the pillar of humility daily. First, treat all of your colleagues with respect—from your boss to the person who empties your garbage can. Second, volunteer when needed—no matter your title, you are never too important to help another person. Lick a few envelopes and provide directions to restrooms. Fundraisers who are humble and say "thank you" will inevitably get to say those words (*thank you*) more often!

> *Have the humility to learn*
>
> *from those around you.*
>
> —John C. Maxwell

Chapter Seven

The Sixth Pillar: Patience

The years teach much

which the days never know.

—Ralph Waldo Emerson

It is generally agreed that the golden rule of real estate is "location, location, location." If there were a golden rule of fundraising, I believe it would be "Patience, patience, patience." All fundraisers—especially those who focus on planned and principal gifts—sometimes need to embrace a longer timeframe on the path to a gift. Donors make gifts when it is best for them, and not necessarily by the end of a calendar or fiscal year, or within your campaign or personal timeline. By practicing patience, you are a more effective fundraiser today than you were yesterday, and you will be more effective tomorrow.

Over time as you meet with a variety of donors, you will hear an assortment of reasons why they were inspired to give. This builds perspective and provides you with a cache of stories that you can share, in turn, with prospective donors.

One of my family members once asked me, "Why do people give to charity? Charity begins at home." When we send a mailing to a large group of patients (or graduates, or members) we know that there are some people who just do not wish to give. Some of them do not value or understand the purpose of giving. And some cannot afford to give.

As a gift planner I have been responsible for the administration of estates of donors who have passed away. Sadly, many have never been thanked for their gifts. Collectively we don't know in advance about the majority of gifts we will receive in this way. This is yet one more reason why it's important for all fundraisers—regardless of title—to ask all of their donors if they have included or would consider including a gift in their wills. When the answer is "yes" we can thank them. And then we can patiently await the gift.

When a gift comes under scrutiny in the judicial system, the results are not always in line with the donor's intent, nor are they always good for nonprofits. There are judges who will rule in favor of even distant family members in litigated will contests. These judges cannot comprehend that someone would choose to make a gift to a charity over family—even when the "family" is a grandniece who lives three thousand miles away, who hasn't seen her great-aunt in forty years, does not know her great-aunt's birthday, and has not had any type of relationship with her great-aunt.

The charity, on the other hand, has received gifts from this donor over many decades. Representatives from the charity have visited with the donor to thank her, invited her to events which she proudly attended, exchanged birthday and holiday cards, and expressed thanks in numerous other ways. Sadly, this patience may not be rewarded, and good stewardship of the donor may not save the gift from being redirected by others who were not familiar with this donor's goals and wishes.

Patience is Caring

Patience has several definitions. The two definitions that most closely fit the pillar of patience for successful fundraisers are, according to Dictionary.com: (1) "quiet, steady perseverance; even-tempered care; diligence" and (2) "an ability or willingness to suppress restlessness or annoyance when confronted with delay." Setting aside the annoyance factor, what I like most in the definition is the word "care." Being patient means that you care enough about the donor to wait until tomorrow to achieve what you want to achieve today. You put your donor's goals precisely where they belong—ahead of your own.

We can learn to be patient. And sometimes we have no choice. Patience improves with maturity and the wisdom gained over time from being a fundraiser. Our coffers of patience will be depleted and replenished as we receive some gifts and wait for others. All fundraisers who have spent time in the trenches have dipped into their patience reserves when needed.

Learning the Hard Way

I have learned when to push someone a bit, and when to back off and give a prospective donor more space. Unfortunately, I learned the hard way.

Earlier in my career I was intensely focused on meeting my metrics. One metric required me to meet with a certain number of donors each month. (This is a popular metric for many fundraisers today.) On one trip I needed to schedule one more meeting. I called a couple who on paper seemed to have a great affinity for my organization. So it came as a surprise when they said "no" to my request to meet. I pushed a bit and I suppose even nagged them for a meeting. Finally, they relented.

I still recall how truly uncomfortable this visit was. They put a chair in the middle of a large common room, sat across the room from me, and asked: "What do you want?" They answered questions in monosyllables and divulged very little. I never pushed (to that extent) again. Nor am I aware that they ever made a gift.

Gift planners, in particular, are viewed as needing—and often having—abundant reserves as they hone this pillar and await gifts which will be received in future years from donors' estates.

Planting Seeds of Patience

Robert Louis Stevenson said, *"Don't judge each day by the harvest that you reap but by the seeds that you plant."* Fundraisers plant many seeds. A seed doesn't become edible fruit in a few days—some seeds take months or even years of sun and rain to ripen. By analogy, it takes time to hone relationships with donors to the harvest time when the donor is ready to make a gift.

The path to a gift is analogous to a hike in a national park. Few trails are laid in a straight line from the starting point to the destination. While sometimes we may wish the path was a little more direct, while we wish we could see around the corner, while we may wish to speed up the journey, it is only by

---

Practicing Zen in an un-Zen Environment

"So, Alex, when are we getting the gift?"

All fundraisers are asked The Question. Some more often than others. And we are expected to give The Answer: "Today, boss!" The Question is often followed by The Second Question: "How much are we getting?"

The most un-Zen part of our jobs is this constant inquisition about the timing and amount of gifts. But we are hired to bring in money for our nonprofits. Some gifts will come. Other gifts take longer, some will not be received this year, and a few won't be received at all. This reminds me of Wendy's "Where's the Beef?" television commercial from years ago. How do we keep a constant flow of Zen in a "Where's the Next Gift" environment?

Even as our bosses continue to ask The Question, we need to keep in mind that they, in turn, are being asked this question. Our response, our job, is to ascertain when the gift is coming in and to be honest about the timing. It may be especially difficult when our answer (after due diligence) is (a) "I don't know," or (b) "Next year," or (c) "After the death of his wife."

Having to wait for a gift is a common occurrence, especially when your gifts are larger, blended, or planned gifts that take time to plan and execute, let alone to be realized or received.

walking all those steps, dodging roots and following the zigzagging path, that we arrive at the top and can enjoy the lovely view.

So, too, is the journey to a gift indirect at times. Few gifts happen in a single transaction. In Zen parlance, *the gift comes when it comes.* We need to stay on the path and remain focused on the destination. Great fundraisers learn to remain focused. Successful fundraisers also learn to savor the journey.

Dogs appear to be patient creatures. Ferguson deserves an award for patience as he often waits up to an hour after I ask him if he would like to go for a walk while I am doing "one more thing." Eventually we go for a walk. Sometimes I even take him for a ride. In gift terms, this is like a gift of $10 million when you are expecting only $1 million! Ferguson—like most dogs—enjoys the ride as much as the final destination—if not more. Most dogs leap into the car, stick their heads out of the windows, hang their tongues out, and smile broadly. Most fundraisers relish the final destination—often viewed as the receipt of the check—and simply cope with the journey. I challenge you to move back the moments of (en)joy to an earlier point in the gift journey. Practice enjoying the walk... and the ride.

> *Trees that are slow to grow*
>
> *bear the best fruit.*
>
> —Moliere

Chapter Eight

The Seventh Pillar: A Sense of Humor

> *If money makes the world go round,*
>
> *it's humor that keeps it from*
>
> *spinning out of control.*
>
> —Craig Kimberley

By now you are familiar with six of the eight pillars that make you a successful fundraiser. The seventh pillar—a sense of humor—is the key to success over time, and one that no successful fundraiser can do without.

A humorous and true story—one apparently not limited to me—involves a donor who asked me for assistance in writing a thank-you note to a vice president for the kind treatment over the course of a weekend that celebrated donors and their generous gifts. I spent a few hours both on the phone with the donor and afterward writing the note from her perspective.

A few weeks later a copy of the letter (which I largely wrote) ended up on my desk with a note from the VP to "please draft a reply." So I proceeded to write the other half of the letter-pair. (A common first-year law school exercise is to prepare to present one side of a controversial issue. Just before presenting to your classmates, the professor tells you to take the opposing view. The goal is to understand the situation from both sides. Little did I know this exercise would foreshadow my duties as a fundraiser!)

Gift planners are a subcategory of fundraisers who I believe particularly need to hone a sense of humor. Although attorneys probably tolerate more

Find the Humor!

A book that I keep on my shelf entitled *I Died Laughing* contains a wonderful selection of humorous stories that touch upon death. This book is special to me because a donor in his nineties gave it to me with the expressed wish that it would help me do my job better. When he first called me, he told me precisely what gift he wanted to make, if I would listen to him. He had a great sense of humor and laughed as he described some of his contemporaries who often say, "If I die…" (Spoiler alert: it's not "if" but "when.") I have used the stories and quotes from this book often throughout my career.

jokes at their own expense, gift planners are teased about "death and taxes," "sending in the grim reaper," and being on the "eradication team." All fundraisers—and especially gift planners who were formerly attorneys—should have a response ready for the inevitable question, "Why (in the world) did you choose to become a fundraiser?" These moments present a good opportunity to take three deep breaths and reset.

> *I think the next best thing to solving a problem is finding some humor in it.*
>
> —Frank A. Clark

Fundraising can be viewed as a solution to a multipart problem. Some donors have too much money and don't wish to give it all to their children. Others have no family to give their estate to. A donor may be inspired to give for a number of reasons but may need guidance in deciding on the allocation or in structuring the gift. Some donors are advised by their accountants to make a gift to gain an income tax deduction.

I recall having dinner with a couple who had expressed an interest in making a gift and receiving a fixed income stream for life. (Some readers may have heard of this technique, a charitable gift annuity.) We were eating dessert—chocolate was the group favorite—and unrealistically stating our hope that the delicious dessert was calorie- and fat-free! I spent two hours with this lovely couple. I wanted to wrap-up our meeting by establishing their continuing interest in making a gift. I asked them to imagine being able to eat more chocolate while losing weight. In other words, to achieve multiple goals. We all laughed. Then I admitted that although this is not feasible, their goals to make a gift and receive an income stream were possible. I left with their request to send updated information and their intention to make a gift by the end of the year.

Humorous Situations

Some situations that can help hone our sense of humor include the following:

- ◆ Having an advanced degree or two and being asked to work at an event where your role is to greet people and answer the question, "Where is the restroom?"

- ◆ Visiting with a donor in his hospital room and offering assistance, which soon comes in the form of helping to cover the patient as his gown falls to the floor.

Six Reasons Donors Are Motivated to Give

I was asked to write an article for a trade publication for estate planning advisors about the reasons people are motivated to make gifts. I shared these six reasons:

Gratitude

Many donors are thankful for the support they or their family received and choose to give back to the same or a different charitable organization.

Religious Mandate

Religion is the top reason donors have made gifts since this began to be tracked in 1972.

Altruism

Giving is part of the American culture and is considered a noble and unselfish action.

Set an Example

Giving is viewed as a way to pass values to the next generation, and by the wealthy as a family tradition.

No Choice

Sometimes a sense of obligation, guilt, or peer pressure results in a gift.

Benefits

Most are familiar with the tangible benefits (such as an income tax deduction or business referrals). However, the intangible benefits (such as achieving a lifelong dream or helping another human being) often trump the tangible benefits.

Brovey, Alexandra P. "My Client, a Donor? Six Reasons That Motivate People to Make Charitable Gifts." *Trusts and Estates*. October 2013.

- Offering to treat a donor to dinner and agreeing to move the time back two hours to 4:30 p.m. to get the "dinner special." At the termination of the meal as the waiter comes to collect payment, the donor springs to life and adds a "2-for-1" coupon into the bill folder, with a big smile.

- Responding to an annual donor's request for information about a gift in the donor's will, only to have the donor call later and ask why we don't want the gift now while he is alive.

- Speaking in front of a group of accountants who answer the question, "Why do people give?" with the (obviously incorrect) answer, "To get a tax deduction." I kept a straight face and educated this key group of advisors about the top reasons people give according to recent studies: to support the mission, to make a difference, gratitude, etc. For six common reasons, see the sidebar.

Sometimes a situation calls for one of two reactions: disbelief, which is usually (and unfortunately) followed by vocal disapproval, or finding something humorous in the situation. The latter enables us to view the situation in light of the bigger picture and draw upon our perspective.

We began the chapter with a quote about money. While money is necessary, it is merely a means to an end. To be successful, we need to be able to laugh at situations. And at ourselves.

> *Imagination was given to man*
>
> *to compensate him for what he is not;*
>
> *a sense of humor to console him*
>
> *for what he is.*
>
> —Francis Bacon

Chapter Nine

The Eighth Pillar: Being a Mentor

> *Confidence, like art, never comes from having all the answers;*
>
> *it comes from being open to all the questions.*
>
> —Earl Grey Stevens

Great mentors have a special secret: they never cease to be students. I practiced being a mentor as I studied toward my black belt in Shotokan karate. Even though I had (and still have) much to learn, I was expected to teach lower belt students.

A mentor is defined as "a wise and trusted counselor or teacher." One interesting fact about mentors is that they don't exist solo; they are one-half of a pair. To be labeled a mentor, you must have a mentee. A teacher requires a student.

We can all learn—and continue to learn—from donors, from our mistakes, and from each other. We can learn from audiences when we speak, and from colleagues with expertise in other areas. Just as parents can learn from their children, so, too, can you learn from your mentees and others of all experience levels.

> *When the teacher is absent, there is no learner, just as when the learner is absent, there is no teaching. When the teacher learns nothing from the student, nothing has been taught. When the learner finds a teacher who listens, both always learn something.*
>
> —*PhDeath: The Puzzler Murders,* James P. Carse, p. 340 (2016).

This quote has several takeaways. First, it recognizes the importance of listening, our second pillar. Second, it shows the mutually beneficial relationship between mentor and mentee. In true Zen fashion, the mentor needs the mentee to make the relationship successful. Either both parties benefit, or neither benefits.

Mentors Are Multifaceted

Great mentors have many answers. But they also continue to ask questions. The Anishinaabe people have the Teachings of the Seven Grandfathers. The first one is: "To cherish knowledge is to know Wisdom." Mentors cherish gaining more knowledge, which over time becomes wisdom. It's somewhat ironic that those whom you would expect to have many of the answers continue to ask questions.

Zen masters often answer a question with a question. (So do psychotherapists, but I'll leave that for another author's book.)

One way to hone your mentorship skills is somewhat counterintuitive: consider ceding some of your training time to a colleague. Mentors use their resources wisely. Key resources include colleagues, advisors, and donors who can describe a gift from a different point of view. Perhaps this alternative point of view is one that another colleague, donor, or advisor can more easily relate to.

Great mentors are also great storytellers. Julia Campbell wrote a book recently published by CharityChannel Press entitled, *Storytelling in the Digital Age: A Guide for Nonprofits*. Storytelling is a very effective way to gain support and keep donors engaged. Sharing stories about the impact of a gift touches an emotional chord in others. A prospective donor who can relate to a story may make the next inquiry that leads to a gift.

Mentors and Inverse Mentors

Even if you are a mentor to others, you may seek a mentor during your career as you develop new skills. Zen permits you to be a mentor and a mentee simultaneously. Practice the pillar of compassion, and put yourself in the shoes of someone who needs a mentor. *What are you seeking?*

Many nonprofits and organizations have mentorship programs. If your nonprofit does not have one, consider starting one by serving as a mentor. Even without a formal program, you can serve in this role.

Most of us have had at least one good mentor. I count myself among the very fortunate to have had a few great mentors. I have also had some "inverse mentors" who taught me a few things. Some of my best lessons came from my observations of what others were doing. Upon reflection I realized those actions were not best practices that I should emulate. While I am not suggesting you intentionally choose an "inverse mentor," you will find yourself working with them, reporting to them, and spending time in their presence. My advice is to make the best of the situation and learn something from them.

Even after two decades as a gift planner, I am fortunate to find mentors with more experience. I seek those who have been in the field for three or four decades. Find a person who you believe can mentor you. Technically you do not even need permission—you can be a "stealth mentee."

If you can be a stealth mentee, you can also be a "stealth mentor." Throughout my career I identified a few colleagues who I sensed would be great partners in soliciting blended gifts for several key areas. I sat with these colleagues at meetings whenever possible, emailed them to discuss prospects and ideas, and responded quickly whenever they called. I invited one colleague to present a training with me about a gift we closed together. The colleague never realized that I was covertly serving as a mentor.

And I'll never tell.

Donors as Mentors

Donors can teach us so much—not only about themselves and the gifts they wish to make—but also about how to be more effective fundraisers. Donors can teach us to think of fundraising in fresh ways. At one nonprofit I received a phone call from a prospective donor in response to a letter that outlined an increase in scholarship levels in coming months. The donor is a dentist whose father was also a dentist; both graduated from the same educational institution. The donor thought of a wonderful gift: he would begin to fund a scholarship annually for five years and include a gift in his will to establish an endowed scholarship fund. He asked me to write a letter wishing his father a Happy Father's Day—his incentive for the timing of this gift—and describing the gift. What a wonderful and creative idea.

Mentors are human like you and me. They don't possess a secret skill set that results in every donor saying "yes" to a solicitation. Think about the times when you prepared and then asked a donor for a gift. And you received the answer "no." How could this happen? *To me?* Months or even years later you may reflect on this non-gift. While you may have been disappointed at the time, some of these "nos" are great learning opportunities. They could also be among your most memorable lessons as a fundraiser. They enhance your ability to be a mentor if you learn something from the experience. Perhaps the lesson is simply to move on.

Mentors possess many of the pillars described in this book. Listening, compassion, and patience are like the bones and muscles that comprise the core of great mentors. Plus, having to explain something more than once or more than one way is the best way to practice for discussions with your prospects and donors.

> *Thousands of candles can be lit from a single candle,*
>
> *and the life of the candle will not be shortened.*
>
> *Happiness never decreases by being shared.*
>
> —The Buddha

Chapter Ten

Summary and Inspiration

All ends are also beginnings.

We just don't know it at the time.

—Mitch Albom

Many of us are familiar with the fundraising cycle. It begins when a donor makes a small, annual gift (usually cash), then with cultivation makes successive gifts, then at some point steps up to make a major gift, then commits to an ultimate gift—a planned gift in the donor's estate. With good stewardship, the donor may repeat the cycle with annual gifts, and may be inspired to make additional major and planned gifts.

In this cycle, each gift represents both an ending and a beginning. The gift is the end result of a donor's response to a solicitation. After the gift is received, the thanks begin, and the gift proceeds can begin to be used as the donor directs.

According to an application of Zen concepts, we are in every gift we assist donors in making. Thank goodness—because until I win the lottery, I will have to be content fulfilling at least some of my philanthropic goals vicariously through my donors!

Most fundraisers' careers are not linear. The path to success (in fundraising and in life) is seldom direct. When I think of my career, I am reminded of the Chartres Labyrinth which is named after the cathedral in France. This popular pattern twists and turns and takes you close to the center. Just when you think you have arrived, the path sends you back. A labyrinth is not a maze, however, so if you persist and continue to follow the path, you will

This is my miniPath© by Relax4Life that I occasionally trace in between activities to "reset" my mind. It gives me a small sense of achievement and helps me find my Zen.

reach the center. When you do reach the center, however, like reaching the summit of Mt. Everest, you are "halfway home."

Those who are new to fundraising might believe that veteran fundraisers have experienced every situation and always know precisely what to do. However, just like an ocean can be calm or choppy, clean or polluted, refreshing or freezing, so do our prospects and donors present all kinds of interesting and unique situations. Some nuances and emotions can challenge even the most experienced fundraiser. Even after two, three, or four decades as a fundraiser, you will still experience new scenarios and interact with new donors.

Picture yourself twenty-five years from now (or, alternatively, picture yourself at age seventy-five). You receive a phone call (or the then-equivalent of this) from someone at your favorite nonprofit. You likely do not know this person, but the voice sounds cheerful and the person speaks clearly. (You don't want to admit it, but you are getting a bit hard of hearing.) The person thanks you for your recent gift and for the gifts you have made over the years. Your experience tells you that the person called for a reason, and you are likely going to be asked for something. How do you feel about this organization? How do you feel about the person who called, at this moment?

This is an exercise in putting ourselves in others' shoes. We do not have to wait until we are retired before thinking about this situation and where giving to our nonprofit fits into the larger plan. If we understand what motivates our donors, we will be more effective fundraisers.

We save lives. We feed the hungry. We educate future generations. We house the homeless. We seek and find cures to diseases. We bring a smile to a sick child. We comfort those in their final days. The community of fundraisers is like a warm blanket, there when you need it—for an answer to a question, to compare results, to share a story or a concern. Together we can share knowledge. And together we are wiser.

Ten Lessons I Have Learned from My Donors

I would like to conclude this book with ten lessons I have learned from my donors:

#1 To Appreciate Receiving a Birthday Card...Without Money in It

Imagine that all of your relatives—parents, grandparents, and siblings—have passed away, you have never married or are widowed or divorced, and you have no children. How many birthday cards will you receive at age ninety? If you are a member of my legacy society, you will receive at least one. Assuming you don't have memory problems, you will likely remember and appreciate this card, and the organization that it represents. You may even remember the person who sent it to you. Hopefully these positive memories reinforce the gifts you have made and will make you smile.

#2 To Be Persistent

Donors often have to speak with multiple people to get an answer to a question or to find the right person who can assist them. And unless you are the first person to hold your position, your donors have likely spoken with your predecessors. This persistence should be rewarded with patience and a response that acknowledges the donor's efforts, and hopefully provides an answer to the donor's question.

#3 To Be Thankful for Life and to Be Able to Give

I have had the privilege of meeting a few Holocaust survivors. I confess my ability to empathize is sorely tested in their presence, but I do rely on the pillar of compassion. One donor, in particular, made a childhood vow to help others if he survived. He survived, thrived, and was generous in life and after that through his estate.

#4 To Embrace Anonymity and Decline Publicity

The highest form of giving in several religions is anonymous giving. Donors who request anonymity choose to step outside the realm of public recognition. Gifts are not made to compete or with any expectation of thanks in return—but simply to help create a better world.

#5 To Appreciate a Week Without a Single Appointment

Gift planners in particular call upon older people to schedule visits. Often if the person has an appointment scheduled anytime during the week—say, Thursday afternoon—the person is inexplicably unavailable for a thirty-minute visit earlier in the week—say, Tuesday morning! All kidding aside, older people visit a number of medical specialists, plus they also enjoy going to lunch, visiting family—especially grandchildren, going to the gym, and playing Mah Jongg and bridge. They welcome "down time," and a visit with a fundraiser might not fit that definition. Hone your pillars of patience and compassion. Call back another time.

#6 To Value a Person over a Title

Professor Russell James has done some research about titles and how prospective donors view them—which is with some level of confusion. "Why is a 'principal' or 'special' or 'strategic' gift officer calling me or coming to see me?" I shared earlier that most of my donors do not know I am a graduate of Georgetown Law and many will not know I wrote this book. What they do value are the qualities portrayed by the pillars—being a good listener, being compassionate, and being patient. They also still value handwritten notes in this digital age.

#7 To Decline an Invitation

My donors may also be your donors and boy are they busy! They get invited to a multitude of lunches, dinners, meetings, and galas. It is wonderfully freeing for them sometimes to say "no" when they simply lack the energy or inclination to participate. Remember that a donor's "no" to an invitation is not "no" to a relationship or "no" to a future gift. Try again another time.

#8 To Volunteer on a Major Holiday

Some volunteers—who also became donors due to their devotion to their nonprofits—kindly volunteer on holidays they do not observe to enable others to spend time with their families. Being unselfish is refreshing and benefits humanity.

#9 To Be Proud of My Age

As charitable gift annuitants know, the older you are, the higher your annuity rate. It's a privilege to live to be ninety- or one hundred-something. Most of my donors have shared their birthdays with me, and in return receive birthday cards—and my profound respect.

#10 To Fulfill a Childhood Promise

There is a subset of donors who were touched by a charity or a stranger's generosity at an early age, and who made promises to themselves to "repay the debt" when and if they could. What an accomplishment to live a good life and to fulfill that promise! The circle of life can be that much sweeter, not only for that donor but also for all who will benefit from the seed planted by the original donor's generosity.

Is the World a Better Place?

At the beginning of the book, I challenged you to differentiate between your largest gift and your most meaningful gift. I introduced the concept of Zen and the need to focus—or be mindful—when meeting with donors. I wonder—and ask you—whether mindfulness and focus increase with the size of the gift? Be honest: even if you believe you have mastered all eight pillars, does your heart beat faster when more zeros are added to the gift size? Mindfulness teaches us that even as we recognize that our hearts do beat faster, we do not judge.

For what I hope is not the final time, please relax and take three deep breaths. And consider perusing my Meditation for Fundraisers.

> **Meditation for Fundraisers**
>
> Take three deep breaths, inhaling and exhaling slowly.
>
> May I be happy.
>
> May I be peaceful.
>
> May I be thankful.
>
> Happy I can help others do good things.
>
> Peaceful knowing I can help others find peace of mind.
>
> Thankful that I can help make the world a better place.
>
> May I learn patience.
>
> May I develop compassion.
>
> May I find wisdom.
>
> Patience to weather excuses, hurdles, and delays.
>
> Compassion to enhance my ability to think outside of my own thoughts.
>
> Wisdom gleaned from experience and passed on to others.
>
> May I walk alongside my donors and, for a few special moments, tread the same path for the benefit of humanity.

Making the World a Better Place

Hopefully you are proud of your career as a fundraiser. The next time you have a quiet moment, ask yourself, "Is the world a better place because I am a successful fundraiser?"

> I can respond "*Yes!*"
>
> I hope you can, too.
>
> *I know what I have given you.*
>
> *I do not know what you have received.*
>
> —Antonio Porchia

Appendix

Books

Campbell, Julia. *Storytelling in the Digital Age: A Guide for Nonprofits.* CharityChannel Press, 2017.

Carlson, Lisa. *I Died Laughing: Funeral Education with a Light Touch.* Upper Access Inc., 2010.

Carse, James P. *PhDeath: The Puzzler Murders.* Opus Books, 2016.

Covey, Stephen R. *The 7 Habits of Highly Effective People: Powerful Lessons in Personal Change.* Free Press, 1989.

Hahn, Thich Nhat. *The Art of Communicating.* Unified Buddhist Church, Inc., 2013.

Hanh, Thich Nhat. *The Art of Living.* Unified Buddhist Church, Inc., 2017.

Livio Mario. *Why: What Makes Us Curious.* Simon & Schuster, 2017.

Meyers, Steven L. *Personalized Philanthropy: Crash the Fundraising Matrix.* CharityChannel Press, 2015.

Pirsig, Robert. *Zen and the Art of Motorcycle Maintenance: An Inquiry Into Values.* HarperTorch, 1975.

Prentiss, Chris. *Zen and the Art of Happiness.* Power Press, 2006.

Stanley, Thomas J. and William D. Danko. *The Millionaire Next Door: The Surprising Stories of America's Wealthy.* Taylor Trade Publishing, 2010.

Wohlleben, Peter. *The Hidden Life of Trees: What They Feel, How They Communicate.* Greystone Books Ltd., 2015.

Articles and Presentations

Brovey, Alexandra. "Black Belt Gift Planning: Ten Stages to Becoming a Master." National Conference on Philanthropic Planning. Orlando, Florida, 2015.

Brovey, Alexandra P. and Patricia L. Roenigk. "How Old Are You and Did You Know You Could: Initiating Planned Gift Discussions and Getting Answers to Key Questions." National Conference on Planned Giving. Denver, Colorado, 2008.

Brovey, Alexandra P. "My Client, a Donor? Six Reasons That Motivate People to Make Charitable Gifts." *Trusts and Estates.* October 2013.

"Mindfulness: The New Science of Health and Happiness." *Time Special Edition.* Time Inc. Books, 2017.

"The Making of Genius," *Time,* November 27/December 4, 2017.

Websites

Bible.com

Dailyzen.com

Dictionary.com

Literarydevices.net

Miriam-Webster.com

Relax4Life.com

Index

A

accountants, 41, 43
annuity, charitable gift, 9, 41
attorneys, 16, 29, 39, 41
  estate planning, 7, 13
  nonprofit's, 31

B

Bible, 17, 22
brain work, 18
breathing, 5
breaths, 3, 5, 16
  deep, 4–5, 14, 22, 32, 41, 53–54
Buddha, 31, 48
Buddhism, 22

C

careers, 2–3, 6, 16, 21, 29, 31, 35, 40, 46–47, 49, 54
charitable gift annuitants, 53
CharityChannel Press, 46
compassion, 4, 21–23, 48, 52, 54
  acts of, 24
  pillar of, 46, 52
conversation, 8–10, 17–19
Covey, Stephen R., 16
cultivation, 11–12, 49
cultivation phase, 12
curiosity, 2, 4, 25–28
Curious George, 25, 28

D

deep breathing, 4–5
donor cycle, 11
donor-focused fundraising, 7
donors, 4, 6–19, 21–28, 30–36, 39–43, 45–54
  multiple, 14
  new, 50
  older, 16
donor's goals, 7, 17, 23, 34
donor's intent, 34

E

Einstein, Albert, 25, 28
energy, 17–18, 53
estate planning advisors, 42
estates, 7, 33, 36, 41–42, 52
  donor's, 31, 49

F

families, 16, 31, 34, 41–42, 52–53
Ferguson, 2, 13
fundraisers, 2–5, 7–8, 10, 13, 19, 26–30, 32–37, 39, 41, 48–54
  effective, 33, 47, 51
  excellent, 2, 25
  experienced, 50
  successful, 2, 8, 26, 34, 37, 39, 54
  veteran, 50
fundraising, 2, 6–7, 12, 29, 33, 41, 47, 49–50

G

gift planners, 33, 36, 39, 41, 47, 52
gift planning, 17
gifts
  annual, 49
  anonymous, 32
  blended, 27, 47
  endowed, 27
  largest, 6, 27, 53
  legacy, 19, 27
  major, 7
  meaningful, 6–7, 53
  multiple, 6
  planned, 17, 36, 49
  six-figure, 9
  ultimate, 49
goals, 5, 7–9, 16, 22–23, 26–28, 39, 4
gratitude, 13, 42–43
greatness, 30

H

humility, 4, 29–32
humor, 39–41
  sense of, 4, 39–41, 43

J

journey, 10, 13, 36–37
joy, 8, 10–11, 37

L

listening, 4, 15–19, 22, 46, 48, 52

M

Master, Zen, 3, 46
meetings, 4, 10–11, 17–18, 21, 23, 26, 35, 41, 47, 52–53
mentee, 45–46
  stealth, 47
mentors, 4, 26, 45–48
  inverse, 46–47
  stealth, 47
mentorship programs, 46
mindfulness, 3, 8, 11, 14, 53

P

patience, 2, 4, 33–37, 48, 52, 54
Personalized Philanthropy: Crash the Fundraising Matrix, 17
prospective donors, 10, 12, 26–27, 33, 35, 46–47, 52

R

relationships, 11, 19, 26, 28, 34, 46, 53

S

skills, 2–4, 8, 17–18, 23
solicitation, 4, 11–13, 47, 49

Z

Zen, 3–5, 7, 22–23, 36, 46, 50, 53
Zen concepts, 8, 11, 49
Zen Master, 3, 46
　Thich Nhat Hanh, 16

Did You Enjoy This Book?

If you enjoyed this book, we have great news! ***Zen and the Art of Fundraising: 8 More Pillars of Success*** is slated for publication in late 2018.

It's available at:

https://charitychannel.com/professional/zen-art-fundraising-8-pillars-success.

Did you know that CharityChannel Press is the fastest growing publisher of books for busy nonprofit professionals? Here are some of our most popular titles.

CharityChannel.com/bookstore

CharityChannel.com/bookstore

CharityChannel.com/bookstore

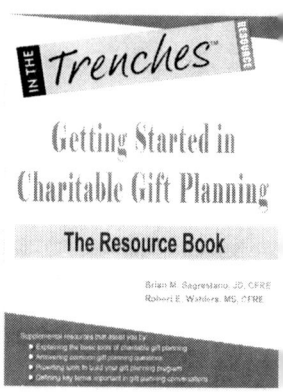

And more!

CharityChannel.com/bookstore

CPSIA information can be obtained
at www.ICGtesting.com
Printed in the USA
FFOW03n1652230318
46017822-46923FF